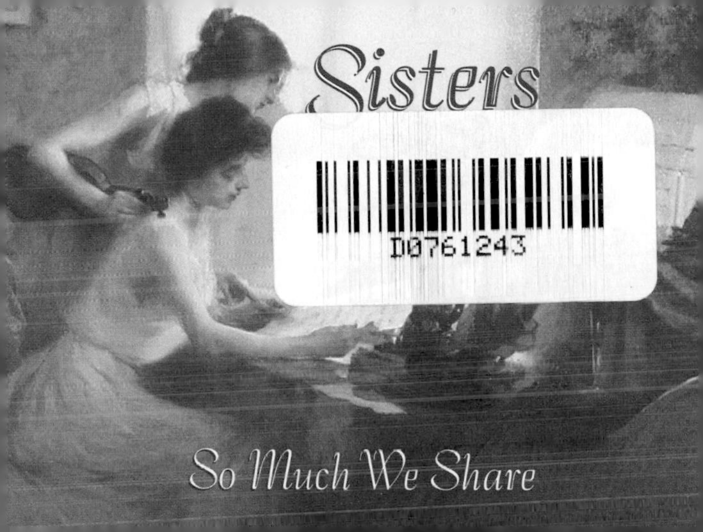
Sisters
So Much We Share

Brownlow Publishing Company
6309 Airport Freeway
Fort Worth, Texas 76117

ISBN 1-57051-051-2

Cover/Interior:
Koechel Peterson & Associates

Printed in USA